BEYOND COINCIDENCE

How Business Leaders Achieve Greatness with Energy Secrets

BEYOND COINCIDENCE

How Business Leaders Achieve Greatness with Energy Secrets

Riddhi Saboo Tahalramani

Available on amazonkindle

Worldwide Published by

Pendown Press
PREMIUM BUSINESS PUBLISHER

PENDOWN PRESS LLP
An ISO 9001 & ISO 14001 Certified Co.,
Regd. Office: 3767A, Kanhaiya Nagar,
Tri Nagar, Delhi-110035
Ph.: 8130886000, 9650072927
E-mail: info@pendownpress.com
Branch Office: 1A/2A, 20, Hari Sadan, Ansari Road,
Daryaganj, New Delhi-110002
Ph.: 011-45794768
Website: PendownPress.com

Edition: 2025
Price: ₹ 299
ISBN: 978-93-6338-647-1

Layout and Cover Designed by Pendown Graphics Team
Printed and Bound in India by Thomson Press India Ltd.

Dedicated to those who dared to
hope again. And to those still learning
to believe in themselves.
This book walks beside you.

CONTENTS

PREFACE

I never thought I'd write a book like this.

For the longest time, I believed that life just "happens" — that some people are lucky, and some are not. But with time, life made me pause, reflect, and ask deeper questions. I saw people smiling on the outside and breaking on the inside. I saw dreams being buried under daily struggles. I saw hope disappearing quietly from people's eyes. And somewhere in all of this... I saw myself.

This book is not written to impress anyone. It is written to connect. It is for people who feel they are doing everything right, yet something feels missing. It is for those who lie awake at night wondering, "When will things change for me?" It is for the ones who silently fight their battles without anyone ever noticing.

You don't need to be rich, educated, or "perfect" to read this. You just need to be someone who's ready to look within and take a small step toward change.

I have written every word with honesty, and with the intention that even if this book can help one person feel lighter, stronger, or more hopeful — then it has done its job.

You're not alone. And you're not stuck.

Maybe... This is your beginning.

With love and faith,

Riddhi

Acknowledgements
A Note From the Heart

Whatever I have achieved in life would have been impossible without the support of my parents and in-laws. They've shown me the meaning of unconditional love, resilience, and grace. I've grown because they believed in me and the wings I have today are because they never held me back. This journey, and every page of it, is as much theirs as it is mine.

To my husband, Bhaveshh, who has stood by me through every twist and turn. Your strength, support, and quiet confidence have been my anchor. Thank you from the bottom of my heart.

To my son Bhiyan, who is my source of happiness and inspiration. Lots of love!

My heartfelt gratitude to all my mentors and guides who have shown me light and direction in times of confusion.

To my team, your commitment, creativity and constant support have played a huge role in making this dream come true. You are the backbone of everything we do, and I feel proud to have you by my side.

A special acknowledgement to Kavita Bakre, my dear friend and the one because of whom this whole journey began.

And finally, to all my loved ones who have been with me on this journey—thank you for your unwavering support, encouragement, and affection. Even if your names are not mentioned, you always hold a special place in my heart.

Without the support of all of you, it would not have been possible for me to move forward with confidence.

Why This Book and Who This Book Is For

This book was born from a simple yet powerful intention — to help people feel lighter, clearer, and more in control of their inner world. Life often gets overwhelming. We carry emotional baggage, limiting beliefs, and silent doubts that slow us down. Somewhere along the way, we forget that we have the power to shift, grow, and rise.

This is not limited to business owners or those deep into personal development. It is written in a manner that **homemakers, working professionals, parents, students, retired elders** – anyone – can read and relate to it. Especially those who have ever felt stuck, lost, or unsure about what's next.

You don't need to know the Law of Attraction or be an expert in meditation. All you need is the willingness to pause, reflect, and try something new.

If you've been asking questions like:

"Why do I feel so low?"

"Why isn't life working the way I want?"

"What is blocking me from moving forward?"

– then this book is for you.

So, let's not wait anymore – turn the page and begin a journey that just might change the way you see yourself and your life.

Chapter 1

ECHOES OF THE PATH: BECOMING ME!

Like many entrepreneurs, my father began his journey with one goal—to give his family a better life. As a first-generation entrepreneur, he spent 20 years in Bombay, traveling to Nagpur twice a week, which was not easy for me as a child.

This impacted me emotionally as I used to miss his presence and the small moments we created together, while he was determined to work tirelessly for us and achieve his goals. As a young girl, I couldn't understand the trade-off. I only knew that I missed my dad. I longed for those small moments — playing together, eating dinner as a family, hearing his voice every night. That emotional absence left a void in me, one that followed me into adulthood.

Until one day, I realized how deeply the emotional patterns that had developed affected my well-being both emotionally and mentally. That void made it difficult for me to connect deeply with others. That was when I decided to work on myself and help others who had encountered similar experiences.

This realization led me to dive deeper into meditation, yoga and exploring Emotional Quotient (EQ). The journey into the realm of mental and emotional well-being gave me the strength to **HEAL and HELP**. The more I believed, the more I healed.

And as I healed, I noticed that I wasn't alone. Everyone — no matter how successful or outwardly confident — is dealing with some emotional wounds. Some are aware of them, many are not. But all of us are, in some way, broken and seeking wholeness.

This awakened my consciousness and the need to help others arose too. Driven by this realization, I began hosting emotional awareness workshops, facilitating community events, and co-founding a BNI network to help entrepreneurs GROW *SUSTAINABLY*. My mission was (and still is) to ensure that success doesn't come at the cost of personal peace or family connection.

Today, with over 12 years of experience, I offer specialized workshops integrating the Law of Attraction, Emotional Mastery, and Non-Violent Communication—designed to help entrepreneurs live abundant, fulfilled lives with time for what truly matters.

This is the very purpose of my life which not only serves as a source of motivation for me to work hard but also provides fulfillment to my soul.

⦸⦸⦸⦸

Chapter 2

THE STORY OF ACCEPTANCE LIFESTYLE CIRCLE

My journey began in 2013 when a seed was planted, and I was introduced to meditation. This gentle spark led me down to a trail where my footprints longed to follow a deep and transformative journey of self-growth and personal development. I found myself completely drawn into books, videos, and teachings on spirituality, emotional intelligence, and the psychology of change. It felt as though the universe had opened a doorway to inner exploration.

By 2016, I launched my first emotional management workshop with a small but deeply engaged group. To my surprise, the impact was significant. As we explored emotional awareness and learned to navigate our inner landscape with clarity and strength, it became evident that emotional mastery isn't just helpful—it's essential. Especially for business leaders, who often find themselves leading from a place of burnout instead of balance, this inner work proved to be a powerful foundation for growth.

I happened to take a few more sessions that year, but life had some other plans to execute. Soon after that time, I immersed myself into the beautiful intricacies of life by launching BNI and Corporate Connections in Nagpur, platforms that allow business owners to connect, collaborate, and grow. Around the same time, I also began a beautiful new chapter of my life-marriage and parenthood. Though my training journey took a backseat, my **learning never stopped**. Each role added a new layer of depth to my personal evolution.

Then came December 2022. I attended the **Enlightened Warrior Power Workshop of T. Harv Eker**, conducted by Success Gyan, and it turned out to be nothing short of magical—powerful, soul-stirring, and awakening. It reignited my passion for training, reminding me that I already held within me a reservoir of powerful content—proven, lived, and deeply resonant. I didn't need to seek outside anymore. The answers were already within.

That's when I founded the **Acceptance Lifestyle Circle** – a nurturing, conscious space for business owners and professionals to grow in emotional awareness, reconnect with themselves, and live more fulfilling, intentional lives. became my mission to help others bridge the gap between success and emotional peace.

A beautiful turning point came when my dear friend and BNI member, **Kavita Bakre** and I were having an amazing conversation regarding **Affirmations** and **Law of Attraction** and how she unknowingly and effortlessly practiced it without being actually aware of the theory behind it. That moment brought clarity as I could see that emotional regulation and manifestations are the two sides of the same coin. I realized how combining emotional management with the law of attraction can help people manage their emotions while manifesting abundance. That's when I saw the synergy: *Awareness meets abundance.*

This was the beginning of something truly magical in my life which helped me find the purpose of life- finding joy in guiding people to manage emotions and manifest abundance to live life with contentment. A life rooted in self-awareness and lived with contentment. Transformation began!

CASE STUDY

The Power of Belief: Aditya's Path to Recovery and Rise

Aditya Deo was told he had NAFLD, which stands for Non Alcoholic Fatty Liver Disease. It is a health problem that usually takes six to ten months to go away. He felt worried and unsure about how long the healing would take or if it would even work.

But after attending the **Law of Attraction workshop,** everything began to change. By using the tools and practices he learned there every day, something amazing happened. In just three months, his doctor confirmed that the disease was fully gone.

Not only did his health improve, but his work life also took a big jump. He started seeing unexpected success and new growth in his career. His journey shows that healing and success can come faster when the mind and body are aligned.

Chapter 3

ALIGNED WITH ABUNDANCE

When abundance comes to our mind, we think it is only meant for a select few lucky people. *But what if abundance wasn't luck at all? What if it was a frequency, and all we had to do was tune in?*

What I want to say is that it is a matter of practicing manifestation to attract abundance. Fulfilling lives, thriving careers, beautiful relationships and a healthy body is what everybody desires but why only some could attract it. WHY? It is because only a few out of everyone try to actually work on the core. *They choose to align their inner world first and everything else follows.* The truth, **abundance** is not a luxury, it is a self-driven choice available to all of us.

Abundance, as I say, is a choice, reflects that only a few people think, act and prepare themselves internally. That makes all the key differences and defines the path of our life. Most of us *want* abundance. DON'T WE? We wish for happiness, wealth and love-but rarely do we work on our mindsets to achieve it and thus miss our chance of getting abundance as a default. It only remains as our desire. I want to affirm that abundance like every other thing must be practiced by cultivating the mindset and developing and nurturing it.

While a common misconception is that abundance is just about wealth and finance, whereas, I would like to correct it and say that abundance not just includes your wealth but it also includes the other dimensions of life-**health, career and relationships too**. Let's cover each dimension in detail in the further chapters.

Health: The Foundation of Everything

If we are not healthy, then nothing else really matters much to us. Health is the foundation of everything. We may have a thriving business or flourishing career but not good health, say a small ailment like headache or knee pain - this can take up a lot of mental and emotional space.

IT REALLY DOES!

So the question here is - do we start taking care of our health when caught with ailment? Ideally, No. If you are currently struggling with health or you want to maintain it. The answer is the same: START NOW! Work and improve upon your health, if you are unwell. If you are good, then start maintaining and strengthening it.

Your body is your only permanent home—nurture it before it starts demanding your attention.

This is the most important pillar of the abundance without which other areas would have no significant meaning.

Career: Fulfillment Over Frustration

Whatever profession you are into - a business owner, a working professional or even a government employee - abundance is not just about having money or wealth. It also carries with itself the aspects like self-fulfillment, growth and joy.

Let's say that, because I am not happy in the business, it is not going to grow. Or the business is not growing so I am not happy. This is like a chicken and egg relationship where one thing is because of another and yet we find no roots of the origin.

Also, reflecting a significant trend in the small business sector, Forbes data reveals that a vast majority, over 80%, of small businesses are solo ventures and managed by the owners themselves thus leaving less time for themselves and their families to spend together. This creates frustration and the reality is far from self-fulfillment. This is a vicious cycle.

To break free, we need to PAUSE. As the snowball gets bigger and bigger if not stopped, so do our negative thoughts if left unchecked.

Relationships: The Invisible Balance

You could have everything in career and health but if your relationships are strained, your life will still feel unbalanced. By relationships, I mean not just romantic relationships but also the relationship you have with your family, friends, team members, clients, or vendors. **Abundance in relationships is the key.**

I remember when Bhaveshh (my husband) and I launched BNI in Nagpur. We worked from 7 AM to 11 PM every single day. Even now we have 2-3 such days a week. It was intense, but we were doing it together, and our parents understood. That helped. But imagine if only one of us had been working those hours, while the other was expecting time together?

No matter how supportive your partner is, they also want to feel connected and valued. The same goes for friendships, team dynamics, and professional relationships. If your staff doesn't feel seen or appreciated, their motivation and efficiency will suffer.

Relationships need NURTURING—**not just attention, but intentional emotional investment.**

Wealth: Not Just Earning, But Growing

Wealth is an important part of abundance and trust me, everyone wants abundance in wealth.

Many people earn well and earn enough, but a lot of them lack financial planning and investment habits, which leads to spending their hard-earned money recklessly. My CA experience speaks loud here.

The deficit in the idea of growing wealth means that money can fulfill your present but may not sustain your future. And thus, abundance in wealth is just as important as growing a business or getting amazing health.

Having abundance in wealth gives your body and mind the fuel to **GO ON** persistently and thus boosts your intrinsic confidence to perform better. Money is energy—and how we handle it reflects how we handle ourselves.

When managed well, it creates peace. When ignored, it creates pressure.

A Life in Balance!

Imagine you are supposed to lay the foundation of a tall building, which requires a strong and steady foundation. And that foundation is determined by the girth, strength and the height of the pillars to be built. If one pillar is too short, or the other one is too tall, will you be able to lay further layers on that uneven base?

Obviously not!

Likewise with our lives. If we lack in any of the pillars—health, career, relationships, or wealth, we may not lay a strong foundation. This imbalance can eventually lead to the collapse of our strong and tall building (our personality and potential) that we aspire to create.

This book is a gentle but powerful step toward **bringing balance across all four pillars**—health, career, relationships, and wealth. Our goal is not to chase abundance, but to live it, every single day, in every single way.

Let's embark on this journey together—with awareness, courage, and a willingness to realign. *Because when you live in alignment, abundance becomes your default mode—not your distant dream.*

CASE STUDY

When Clarity Meets Belief

Jignesh Sable's Breakthrough Story

Jignesh Sable always had a big dream of receiving an event worth over ₹2 crore. The vision was crystal clear in his mind, but the path ahead felt uncertain and overwhelming.

When he joined the 40-day journaling workshop, something began to shift. Each day, he took a few quiet moments to put pen to paper, writing his intention with quiet confidence and growing faith.

At first, it was simply an exercise. But gradually, it turned into a powerful habit. Slowly, his doubts started to melt away and belief began to take root. The consistent practice brought him clarity, sharpened his focus, and aligned his mindset with his goal.

What once felt like a distant possibility started to feel real. He felt more grounded, more intentional, and more in tune with what he truly desired.

And soon after, the very breakthrough he had written about arrived. It felt as though it had been waiting for him to fully believe it was possible.

Chapter 4

VERSION 2.0: POWERED BY PURPOSE

When I reflected on the four pillars of abundance—health, wealth, career, and relationships—I realized that I wasn't always in a balance.

In my young years, my health was okay and wealth was not of much concern. At the age of 17 or 18, truth be told—we rarely think about building wealth. But the two areas where I struggled during those years were career and relationships.

I was pursuing Chartered Accountancy (CA)- not because I wanted to, but because back then, Nagpur had limited options when it came to good colleges. That convinced me that pursuing CA would add value to my career. I loved studying, yes but deep down, I did not want to practice CA.

This mismatch created a silent resentment in me because of which I started blaming my parents for not letting me pursue a different path or study elsewhere. I gradually began to withdraw emotionally, sharing very little with my family. This created a huge emotional gap between me and my parents, leading to strained relationships. I was living a life of lies where I used to lie for even the smallest of the things.

The Turning Point: Silence and Self-Inquiry

During my CA journey, one of my friends re-introduced me to a meditation organization. I had no idea where I was heading—I just knew I needed peace and calmness. I found peace in that silence.

But even then, I found myself complaining and cribbing about things. I was still caught in frustrations, but deep inside, I was realizing that something has shifted. I had found **HOPE**—a quiet, unshakeable feeling that this too shall pass.

I have always found myself a keen reader and so I immersed myself into the world of reading. I started reading books on philosophy and psychology. This not only helped me shape the perspective of the outside world but also about the inner world that lies into me.

To my amazement, one tiny article named *"Power of thought"* changed my life. This was from the same spiritual organization which was regarding the "thought power". It was authored by **Bhramarshi Patriji** and I still remember how it felt. It struck me like a sword. I realized I was being too negative about things in particular and life in general.

"If thoughts pour into my mind– why not be positive instead of negative ones?"

READ IT AGAIN!!

This one thing changed my conscience and then I decided to start small. I read those powerful words every day. I even pasted a copy on my notice board so I could read it every day. Slowly, I was rewiring my mind. **That was the beginning of my mindset shift.**

The Path Reveals Itself

The unknown about this journey led me to step into the "Law of Attraction." After reading that article, I started practicing the art of **attracting the right people, the right workshops, and the right resources.** Most significantly, I started attracting positivity in life gradually.

I remember someone once telling me about a two-day workshop on Emotional Quotient (EQ). It was a small group of about 10–12 participants, but the experience had a profound impact on me. By that time, I was already certain that I didn't want to continue on my current path. But if not Chartered Accountancy, then what? While I didn't have all the answers yet, I was beginning to gain clarity about what I truly wanted to do with my life.

I came across my basic interests of marketing and communication but till then I hadn't come across the right outlet yet. And then came another pivotal moment—I attended a **BNI meeting**. That single step marked the beginning of something much bigger than I ever imagined.

Today, when I look back, I always feel there was a reason that I came across that one particular article on 'Thought Power' which happened to shift my perspective and life and changed it for the good. It helped me see that the life I was living wasn't happening *to* me—it was happening *through* me. Everything that happened in my life was meant to be, not just a coincidence.

And Now...

I remember the journey which began from confusion and chaos to clarity and peace. This taught me that abundance isn't just about extrinsic success but the clarity which leads to achieve this success and attract abundance. Everything starts aligning once you begin working on your thoughts and beliefs.

I thank my younger self who sustained everything back then and my gratitude towards the article is strong enough to justify my emotions.

This book is not just about ideas—it's about living proof. My story is just one example. Yours will be different, but the essence remains: you have more power than you think.

⦸⦸⦸⦸

Chapter 5

REVEALING THE SECRET TOOL

Let's come to a small anecdote this time—to actually reveal the *secret tool* that helped me come out of the confusion and truly start practicing affirmations.

"Whenever a baby elephant is born, it is tied with a rope around one of its legs, usually to a tree or a post. As a baby, the elephant does not have the strength to break free, and no matter how hard it tries, it fails. Over time, the baby elephant gives up trying.

Now, fast forward a few years—this baby grows into a powerful, massive adult elephant, easily capable of snapping the same rope in seconds. But the elephant doesn't even try. Why? Because it *believes* it can't. Its earlier experiences have built a belief that breaking free is impossible."

This is exactly what happens with us. Based on our past experiences, especially the ones that caused discomfort, failure, or rejection, we form beliefs about our capabilities. These beliefs, if left unchecked, become mental ropes that continue to hold us back. Even though we've grown, evolved, and have the strength now, we don't even try—just like that elephant. These are called **limiting beliefs**— and they're often invisible.

But they shape *everything*.

What Are Limiting Beliefs?

Limiting beliefs are those thoughts or inner narratives that restrict our potential. They shrink our confidence, suppress our courage, and lead to a limited mindset. This might have been the result of a real-life experience or something someone said to us, but now they no longer serve us.

Here are a few examples of limiting beliefs people commonly carry:

- "I am too young to get quality clients."
- "I'm not good enough."
- "I don't look good without makeup."
- "I am too beautiful; people won't take me seriously."
- "People like me can't succeed in this field."
- "Once you get a condition like thyroid, it stays for life."

And many small things like these can have a big impact.

Even people who seem confident and put together may quietly harbour such beliefs. Let's say that a beautiful person might have a belief that they cannot step out of their houses without wearing makeup since they may not look good naturally.

How Do They Impact Us?

These beliefs work like auto-pilots. They become our default settings—shaping our mindset, our decisions, and our daily actions. And the most dangerous part? These beliefs happen to limit our growth and we believe in them unknowingly even if these might be far from reality.

Let me share a personal story.

I used to believe that it gets difficult to lose weight once you turn 30. This belief was imbibed into my mind subtly and this is seemingly common among almost all women I met. Not only that, I also had a strong belief that: "Once you get thyroid, it never goes away."

And I am being honest that I was not repeating these thoughts consciously but these beliefs shaped my mindset and influenced me negatively. Because earlier, even with a simple 30-minute walk I could lose weight but now despite everything being done right, I couldn't lose weight. This led me to suffer frustration.

In January 2024, I got tested for thyroid—something someone casually suggested. The results turned positive, though it was borderline. That moment was a realization: I had internalized beliefs that were holding me back. I decided to let go of them and work consciously to rewrite my mindset.

That realization **made me break a belief** by using affirmations for self-belief and focussing on health. I was committed and I could see the result that despite travelling twice a month on an average, eating out five times a week, and working out just three times a week, from January to November 2024, I lost **12 kilograms**. It wasn't magic. It was a mindset.

How Can You Overcome Limiting Beliefs?

It is all about awareness because you need to recognize the beliefs that are controlling your thoughts in the background. You could ask yourself:

- Where did this belief come from?
- How is it impacting me and is it still relevant in the present circumstances?
- Is there someone who might not have this belief and is thriving?

For instance, we might meet someone of our age who is successful but here we are stuck in the same belief that, "I'm too young to get good clients." Do you really think that person holds the same belief? Not really and that is why they could make it so far.

And that alone proves something powerful:

A belief is *not a fact—it's just a perspective.*

CASE STUDY

Finding Peace Within: Ajit Gokarn's Journey

Ajit Gokarn, 73, is a seasoned Chartered Accountant who dedicated over four decades to his profession before retiring in 2019. With a well-planned vision for a peaceful and fulfilling post-retirement life, he looked forward to enjoying hobbies, nurturing social connections and spending quality time with his family.

However, the COVID-19 pandemic disrupted his plans, leading to unexpected emotional struggles. Ajit began experiencing a deep loss of self-confidence, fear of routine tasks, hesitation to step outside, and even difficulty writing or signing his name. Most challenging of all was his inability to share these feelings with anyone, leaving him feeling isolated—despite being surrounded by family.

As the world began to recover, Ajit's internal world remained uncertain—until his daughter, Kavita, introduced him to Riddhi, a Law of Attraction (LoA) practitioner. Alongside psychiatric guidance, yoga, and meditation, Riddhi's sessions gave Ajit a safe and non-judgmental space to express his fears. This marked the beginning of his healing journey.

Through consistent support and inner reflection, he gradually began to understand that affirmations become truly powerful only when backed by a strong, well-nurtured mind. With daily meditation and positive affirmations, Ajit started rebuilding his inner strength—one day, one breath, one step at a time.

Today, Ajit continues his practices with clarity and calm, embracing emotional well-being as a lifelong commitment. He credits his transformation to the unwavering support of his daughter, his mentor, and the professionals who stood beside him during his most vulnerable phase.

His journey is a gentle yet powerful reminder that **healing can begin at any age** and that it's **never too late to reclaim your confidence, restore your inner balance, and rediscover peace within.**

Chapter 6

Unleashing and Manifesting the Energy

What I often say is this—our mind is cultivated in a way that even if 99 things are going right in our lives, we tend to fixate on that one thing which does not go right. AND BOOM!

Suddenly, our energy dips. We're left feeling confused, drained, and defeated—because our focus shifted.

But what if we could shift our focus?

I always believed in attracting positivity through affirmations and manifestation. And to tell you the truth, you too can do it. You just need to shift the focus on the positive things around you, instead of obsessing over what's not working.

You can, to a certain extent, practice this through gratefulness—because the power of gratitude works like magic. And to your surprise, it is not as complicated as you might think. You just need to list down something as simple **ten things you're grateful for** the moment you wake up. This one small act can set the tone for a more positive, grounded, and emotionally balanced day.

Another thing that works wonders is when you take a moment to reflect on the highlight of your day before going to sleep. This helps you delve into the little or big moments that brought joy, peace, or a sense of learning. And guess what? You'll find yourself immersed in those beautiful moments, however big or small they may be. This practice not only ends your day on a high note but also conditions your mind to **seek more of such goodness the next day.**

Now let's take a different instance where we are going for a client meeting not with an apt or complete preparation and there you experience yourself bombarded with challenging questions by your clients. Ahh! It is natural to feel discouraged. But you know you can be aware about the lesson - importance of preparation, perhaps a gap you know you can fill. Documenting those questions and preparing answers could become a valuable resource, not just for yourself but for your future team. This helps us develop our ability to reframe difficult situations.

GRATITUDE

It may seem like a small word, but within it lies a strong and almost magical power. And the beauty of gratitude is that you can apply it across every area of your life:

- **Health:** Let's say you're dealing with a small leg injury, but the rest of your body is functioning well. Acknowledging that balance can bring in healing energy and a sense of appreciation for your body's overall strength.
- **Wealth:** Also on the other hand, if you keep saving a certain amount of money of whatever you earn shows our stability and progress. Indeed, this is something to be proud of!!
- **Career:** If you are able to sustain your work, pay your staff well and keep moving forward—even during uncertain phases—it's a **win-win** situation and a mark of leadership.
- **Relationships:** When you begin to notice and appreciate the people who genuinely nourish your soul—be it your

partner, a family member, or a friend—life feels richer and more meaningful.

The most unique way to be positive is to play with *"affirmation cards"*.

Available here:

Engaging with one card daily- pulling one in the morning or before bed-can set intentions and help attract encouraging thoughts and energies into your life.

So yes, shifting focus from pessimism to optimism is significant in the longer run to nurture positivity. It is also a choice that we make everyday- to notice the light even in the shadows. To be grateful for what is, while gently working through what isn't—yet.

Chapter 7

LIES WE LOVE TO BELIEVE

You know, attracting positivity isn't the real challenge, making it your default mode of living is. And this gets especially tough when your mind is bound by certain myths that silently limit your thinking and choices.

In this chapter, I'll be discussing a few common myths and how you can consciously rise above them.

1. **Myth:** ***"There's never enough time."***

   This has been the most customary myth that we always run short of time and we would never get enough time to do a certain thing. But if you really look into this, you might come across the truth that **time is not an actual issue — clarity and priorities are!!**

   When you align your schedule with what truly matters, you create an abundance mindset around time. Start prioritizing what matters for you and keep a track of what truly is in schedule as per the requirement. Even small shifts in your day can lead to big changes in outcomes.

   We all know one businessman from our city who has multiple flourishing businesses, a great social life, superb health, and so on. And how is it that we are struggling with just one business? That example alone proves it's not the time but how we manage and prioritize it that counts.

2. **Myth: *"Confidence comes from achievements."***

   The next common myth that we possess is that confidence comes from achievements and accomplishments. However, it's the other way around.

   So, in that case, you need to realize that confidence can be built in various ways since it is not inherent. To learn the truth, confidence grows through courage and repetition. And yes, the achievements we possess also leverage our confidence—but they don't define it entirely.

3. **Myth: *"Others have to change for me to have better relationships."***

   You often relate your relationships with others in the form that whatever adjustments are to be made should come from the other side. But this often does not resonate with the fact that relationships improve when you change the way you relate to others.

   However, you can improve our relationships gradually by working on them and by identifying the limiting factor that hinders the growth of our relationship. **Sometimes, a small shift in how we communicate or respond can create a huge emotional ripple.** That's how deeper, more meaningful connections are formed.

4. **Myth: *"Being fit means following strict routines or diets.***

   We often get indulged in the myth that to be healthy, it is important to punish ourselves with strict routines or diets. The truth is a healthy lifestyle is all about balance, consistency and self-care.

   Being fit involves moving your body with joy, nourishing it mindfully, and prioritizing mental well-being through rest, reflection, and emotional hygiene. Fitness is not a punishment; it's a way to love and support your body.

5. **Myth: "Wealth is only about money or luck."**

   This is the most common and misunderstood belief that accumulation of wealth is a matter of luck and money. But to realize, the truth is that acquiring wealth is a persistent result of value creation, aligned action, and mindset.

   How to get the issue resolved is through developing a wealth consciousness, offering real solutions to real problems, and letting money follow your purpose—not the other way around. Wealth flows where value is delivered consistently.

6. **Myth: *"Success requires hustle and sacrifice."***

   Every person in their life wants to have a successful and flourishing career and thus gets willingly ready to sacrifice to reach that level. However, are we really required to sacrifice something in order to be successful and keep hustling all the time? To your surprise, a flourishing business or career is actually built through alignment, strategy, and energy management, not constant exhaustion.

   The most preferred way of getting successful shall include **focussing on what lights you up**, building systems, and nurturing relationships that uplift you. **The truth is, sustainability is smarter than burnout.** When you feel in flow, you grow—naturally and joyfully.

7. **Myth: *"Emotions control us—we just have to react."***

   You become a slave to your emotions if you let them control you and just react accordingly without taking any charge of it. Well, you know what **"Emotions are energy in motion,"** and you can learn to regulate and shift them consciously.

   When we learn how to manage our emotions, we spend less time dwelling on emotions and more time toward other areas of our life. **Emotional intelligence isn't about suppression; it's about navigation.** And the more you master it, the more grounded and empowered you feel.

8. **Myth: *"I'll accept myself once I'm perfect."***

   Everybody goes through this dilemma, "Once I become perfect then I will start loving myself." But this is not how it works. **True love begins by accepting yourself at every stage,** with all your flaws and imperfections with compassion.

   Loving yourself immensely is a gift you can give to yourself by embracing your humanness. Your flaws don't make you broken—they make you real. Growth starts with acceptance, not shame.

9. **Myth: *"People must behave a certain way for me to feel okay."***

   Does it really matter if the other person does not behave or act according to your expectations? Emotionally, you may say yes! Perhaps, in reality, it shall not make a huge impact on you. The acceptance of others begins with **letting go of expectations and the illusion of control.**

   You need to make yourself understand the notion that everyone is on their own path. Focus on understanding, not fixing. When you release judgment, relationships soften naturally and grow with ease.

10. **Myth: *"I can only be happy when things go my way."***

    Most of the time, you may feel reluctant to accept things when they don't happen according to your way. But true peace comes from **accepting life as it is and choosing your response with grace.**

    Happiness is a choice and it is available to you every single day. If you keep accepting and try to work things out in the way you wish (which are under control), surely things will start falling in place one by one and chance by chance.

These common myths which are also our limiting beliefs can be overcome by some efforts which give results life-long. There is no alternative to a positive mindset. It's not just a tool; it's the foundation.

⦸⦸⦸⦸

Chapter 8

THE POWER OF MINDSET - LET'S ACT AND RISE TOGETHER!

Coming on to the final chapter of this book, you can **PAUSE, REFLECT** and bring **TOGETHER** everything you have explored so far. Throughout this journey, you might have seen how deeply your inner world — our emotions, beliefs, and mindset — shapes the reality you experience.

You are here to attract abundance by breaking one limiting belief at a time. That alone is a huge act of courage.

Every principle, every technique, and every story we have discussed points back to one powerful truth: **your mindset determines your life, and manifestation becomes your guiding path.** By manifesting what you want, you create the abundance, followed by the right mindset and taking aligned actions.

From unleashing the power of gratitude to understanding the significance of emotional awareness and managing the emotions and thoughts that redirect your path to abundance and happiness, here my intention is to guide you all to lead a life of self-fulfilment.

On top of that, my core message is that **positivity, belief, and an abundant mindset are non-negotiable ingredients**

for success. This may sound simple, but the impact is profound.

When we look at any successful individual, a sports icon, a genius or a business leader - take an exemplary leader like **Late Ratan Tata**- he was able to not only build business and the strong foundation of his legacy but also touch millions of lives through his humility, integrity, and unwavering optimism.

If you study the lives of such great visionaries, one trait is definitely common- **manifestation and mindset**. Even when things went downhill, they had the ability to face the circumstances with the strength to see hundreds of possibilities in the middle of chaos. And let's not forget—it was never easy for them either. They, too, had to face the failures. But they still spoke about abundance and dreams long before they physically achieved what they had manifested in their minds.

To note that, manifestation and abundance is not only meant for successful people. It's not that people become successful first and then start believing in abundance. It's the other way around:

They believe first, they cultivate an abundant mindset first and **that** leads them towards success.

To be brief about what we shall be doing is that if you want to achieve success in your life, it starts with believing and working on the mindset now, in the present moment. It starts with breaking free from self-imposed barriers and tapping into your fullest potential. It means building positive habits, practicing gratitude, visualizing our goals, and refusing to let fear or doubt guide our decisions.

Also, to be true here, **success is not accidental.**

It is intentional.

It is built, layer by layer, **by aligning your thoughts, feelings, and actions** with the life you desire to live.

I intend to give you the guide regarding the insights and tools to begin with this journey:

1. **Emotional Awareness:** Embracing your real emotions and working on them constantly so that you can control them and not the other way around.
2. **Positive Belief:** Looking for the opportunity to learn in every situation, even during your failures.
3. **Belief in Abundance:** The belief that you can get to the point where you belong and want to manifest your life.
4. **Taking Aligned Action:** Moving forward with clarity, confidence, and purpose.

Everything around you is interconnected. Thus, one aspect shall be seen as aligned to another in some or the other way.

Your emotions fuel your mindset.

Your mindset shapes your actions.

Your actions create your reality.

"Mindset is the real bridge between your inner desires and your external results."

Remember

Success doesn't happen to you.

Success happens because of you.

In the end, the choice is yours:

"Take Charge of Your Life and Attract Abundance

Or

Go With the Flow and Be Disappointed Frequently"

Chapter 9

ABUNDANCE ACCELERATOR!

I believe after reading this book, you might be wondering about *how you get into the intricacies of getting into abundance and "LAW OF ATTRACTION"?*

Well, it is simple; dive into this beautiful yet persistent journey!

You just need to build a strong foundation of mindset, emotional awareness, and manifestation practices. And once that's in place, it's time to take the next step: **accelerating your abundance journey**.

I would like to apprise you about my ***"Abundance Accelerator"*** workshop, which will help you achieve the depth of positivity while attracting abundance in every area of your life - with real world results that you can feel, measure, and celebrate.

The **Abundance Accelerator** can be experienced in multiple formats, depending on what suits your needs best:

- **Hybrid Format:** You can join whenever a live workshop is announced. These sessions are interactive, powerful, and filled with collective energy that multiplies your intent.
- **One-to-One Coaching:** If you prefer personalized guidance, a private one-to-one interaction is available. This allows for deep work customized to your specific goals, blocks, and future aspirations.

- **Retreat Format:** For those seeking an immersive experience, there are retreat-style programs where you can disconnect from your daily routine and deeply connect with your inner abundance. These settings provide calm, clarity, and powerful transformation.

Furthermore, we also host **monthly community meetups** to create a space where you can **RECONNECT, RECHARGE,** and **REALIGN** your energy and intentions alongside like-minded individuals walking a similar path of growth.

"Each of these tools has been thoughtfully created to make your journey smoother, deeper, and more joyful. They serve as reminders that abundance is not just a goal; it's a lifestyle."

If you feel called to accelerate your journey, now is the perfect time to take action.

Let's connect personally, understand your needs, and find the best path for you to thrive.

This is your time. This is your journey. Let's make it powerful together!!!

CASE STUDY

From Scarcity to Healing: Mariyam Hussain's Transformation

For a long time, Mariyam Hussain felt stuck — clients weren't paying, her finances were tight and she was battling a painful eczema condition that doctors had told her couldn't be cured. Nothing seemed to work, and hope was slipping away.

Then, in July 2024, she attended the **Abundance Accelerator** workshop. That one decision changed everything.

With full faith, Mariyam began practicing daily affirmations and gratitude. Soon after, a client who had owed her ₹41,000 suddenly paid ₹10,000. She added healing to her intentions and used Zam Zam water during her practice and within weeks, her eczema began to clear. Eventually, it healed completely.

Then came more unexpected breakthroughs — ₹2 lakh was received from an old client, and others began clearing their dues without her even having to follow up.

On June 20th 2025, while in Mecca, Mariyam reflected on how far she had come: 90% of her debts were gone, and so was her skin condition.

Her story is powerful proof that when you believe deeply, act consistently, and stay aligned, life doesn't just change — it responds with grace and abundance.

Chapter 10

THE SUPPORT RESOURCES

Support Resource 1

Take the Next Step with Focus

You don't have to walk this journey alone.

The Abundance Box

The Abundance Box is a set of carefully selected items meant to help you stay centred, motivated, and aligned with your personal intentions. Whether you're working on personal growth, building mindfulness, or simply trying to bring more positivity into your daily life, this collection serves as a gentle reminder of your strength and potential.

Each item is chosen to support:

- Mental clarity
- Emotional balance
- Spiritual connection

This is about supporting the whole you—mind, body, and spirit—as you move toward a life of abundance.

Support Resource 2

Practical Tools for Emotional Awarenes

The Needs and Feelings Cards are designed to help you better understand and express your emotions. They encourage you to pause, reflect, and connect with what you truly need—helping you approach goals and intentions with greater clarity.

This tool can be especially helpful when:

- You want to improve emotional awareness
- You're working through self-growth or mindfulness
- You want to be more intentional in your daily choices

Understanding your inner state is an important part of building emotional resilience and living with purpose.

Here's how you can access these cards-

Support Resource 3

40-Day Guided Journey

This 40-day journey offers small, daily steps toward meaningful growth. You'll receive short (1–2 minute) audio messages that include clear and practical tasks for the day.

These messages are created to help you:

- Align your thoughts and actions with your goals

- Develop greater self-awareness
- Stay consistent, one day at a time

It's a structured way to build momentum and maintain focus without overwhelm.

Support Resource 4

Monthly Community Gatherings

Growth is more sustainable when shared. These monthly meetups offer a space to connect, reflect, and grow with others on a similar path.

Each session is meant to:

- Deepen your understanding
- Maintain progress through ongoing support
- Offer space for honest sharing—both wins and challenges

These gatherings are about being seen and supported in a non-judgmental space, as you.

WHAT DO WE DO NOW?

BOOK A DISCOVERY CALL

Ready to get started?

Book a **free one-to-one discovery call** with me!

Through this quick and meaningful conversation, I will get to know where you are, where you want to go, and recommend the best way forward- as per your requirement.

Let's bring clarity, direction, and momentum to your journey.

Scan the QR Code or reach out via the contact details below.

contact details: +91 8007669911

Let's connect, your next step begins now!